The Plant-Based

Cookbook

100+ Delicious Vegetarian Recipes
for Beginners to Stay FIT
and HEALTHY having fun!
Including Many VEGAN Recipes!

By

Caroline Lewis

Table of Contents

INTRODUCTION

More and more, recently, people are more careful with their diet: they are concerned about the consumption of healthy foods to provide nutrients to the body, but they are also interested that the **foods are not full of preservatives or additives.** Recently, more and more people are looking for ways to eat less processed foods for many reasons: a **healthier lifestyle** and **more sustainability** for the planet.

These reasons have led people to change their diet into vegetarian, vegan, or to exclude by their diet potentially dangerous foods, like **milk**, **sugar**, or **meat**.

The solution is a plant-based diet!

Eat vegetables, fruits and fiber can provide to your body the right amount of nutrients and help you to have a healthier lifestyle!
A Plant based diet is one of the most easy and complete diet you could follow!

"The Plant-Based Cookbook" contains recipes for each type of people: **busy people, nursing mom, pregnant women, elderly people** and also **kids!**

Are you ready to discover 100 fantastic Plant-Based recipes? So... Let's GO!

1. SWEET POTATO TACOS

Medium/Dairy-free

Preparation time: 10 minutes

Cooking time: 30 minutes

Servings: 6

Ingredients:

- ½ cup sweet potato
- 3 tablespoons of olive oil
- 2 teaspoons of red pepper flakes
- ½ onion, finely chopped
- 1 can black beans, drained and drained
- ½ garlic clove, minced
- 1 can of corn, drained
- ½ cup feta cheese, crumbled
- Salt and pepper to taste

Directions:

Peel and finely slice the sweet potatoes.

Preheat the oven to 425°F. Place a big sheet of aluminum foil on a baking dish bottom.

Put sweet potatoes on the baking sheet. Pour on them 2 tablespoons oil and sprinkle with salt and pepper. Fry for 20 minutes in the oven, sometimes turning each of them. Cook until the sweet potatoes are browned.

Meanwhile, heat in a skillet the remaining olive oil on low. Add the sliced onion and cook for 3 minutes. Add the red pepper flakes, garlic clove and mix. Add the beans and ¼ cup of water. Cook for 5 minutes, often stirring. Add the corn and cook for 10 minutes on low, frequently stirring. Then, remove the mixture from the heat and pour into a bowl. Add feta cheese and mix well.

Once sweet potatoes are cooked, place them in a dish. Use the bean mixture as a sauce. Enjoy!

Nutrition:

- **Calories:** 251;
- **Total fat:** 4 g;
- **Cholesterol:** 94 mg;
- **Fiber:** 2 g;
- **Protein:** 15 g;
- **Sodium:** 329 mg

2. SANDWICH WITH FETA AND AVOCADO

Easy/Dairy-free

Preparation Time: 15 minutes

Cooking time: 10 minutes

Servings: 6

Ingredients:

- 6 Feta Cheese slices
- 2 large avocadoes, peeled
- 5 large boiled eggs
- 6 slices sandwiches bread
- 1 ½ cups arugula
- Salt and pepper to taste
- Juice of 1 lemon

Directions:

Place 1 bread slice on a plate top with arugula, sliced avocado and 1 Feta slice. Cover with sliced egg and season with salt and pepper. Drizzle a bit of lemon juice. Repeat procedure for the remaining ingredients. Enjoy!

Nutrition:

- **Calories:** 310
- **Fat:** 18.2 g
- **Protein:** 21.3 g
- **Sodium:** 383 mg

3. <u>SANDWICH WITH FETA AND APPLE</u>

Easy
Preparation Time: 15 minutes
Cooking Time: 10 minutes
Servings: 4
Ingredients:

- 4 slices of feta cheese
- 1 green apple, cored
- ½ celery stalk, sliced
- 1 shallot, chopped
- 2 tablespoons light mayonnaise
- 8 slices whole-grain bread, toasted
- 4 Lettuce leaves
- Salt and pepper to taste
- Juice of 1 lemon

Directions:

Slice the apple, the celery stalk, and the shallot. Take 1 slice of bread and spread a bit of mayonnaise on a side. Cover with a few apple slices, celery slices, and shallot slices. Cover with feta slices. Season with salt and pepper and drizzle with a bit of lemon juice. Cover with one lettuce leave and top with another bread slice.

Repeat the procedure for the other sandwiches. Serve and enjoy.

- **Calories:** 315
- **Fat:** 11.3 g
- **Carbs. :** 40g
- **Protein:** 15.1 g
- **Sodium:** 469 mg
  Fiber: 3 gr

4. SPICY NACHOS SNACK

Easy/Dairy-free

Preparation Time: 5 Minutes   **Cooking Time:** 15 Minutes   **Servings:** 4

Ingredients:

- 30 tortilla chips
- ½ red onion
- 1 tablespoon of red bell pepper flakes
- 1 medium red bell pepper, sliced
- 1 can tomato salsa
- ½ cup Greek yogurt
- 2 tablespoons black olives
- ½ Jalapeno, sliced

Direction:

Dice the onion, Jalapeno, and red bell pepper. Mix all in food processor with tomato salsa and chopped olives, and blend.

Take a bowl and add the Jalapeno mix and yogurt; then add red bell pepper flakes and mix well. Garnish the tortillas with the sauce on top and serve.

- **Calories:** 238
- **Fats:** 10 g
- **Fiber Content:** 2 g
- **Protein**: 13 g

5. RASPBERRY POMEGRANATE SMOOTHIE

Medium/Gluten-Free/Vegetarian Friendly

Preparation time: 5 minutes

Cooking time: 5 minutes

Servings: 1

Ingredients:

- 2 cups pomegranate juice
- ½ cup coconut milk
- 1 teaspoon vanilla extract
- 2 cups fresh baby spinach
- 1 cup frozen raspberries
- 2 medium bananas
- 2 tablespoons lemon juice
- ½ cup of ice cubes

Directions:

Take a food processor. Add baby spinach, bananas and raspberries and blend for 3 minutes.

Add pomegranate juice, vanilla extract, lemon juice, ice cubes, and coconut milk.

Blend for 5 minutes, until smooth. Serve and enjoy!

- **Calories:** 303;
- **Total fat:** 3 g;
- **Cholesterol:** 0 mg;
- **Fiber:** 2 g;
- **Protein:** 15 g;
- **Sodium:** 165 mg

6. MANGO CONONUT MUESLI

Easy/Dairy-free/Vegan   **Preparation time:** 5 minutes

Cooking time: 0 minutes

Servings: 3

Ingredients:

- ½ cup oat flakes
- ½ cup coconut milk
- 1 tablespoon pure maple syrup
- A pinch of salt
- 1 tablespoon sesame seeds
- 1 tablespoon pumpkin seeds
- 1 teaspoon cinnamon
- ½ cup strawberries, sliced
- ½ cup blackberries, sliced
- 1 mango, stripped, pitted, sliced
- 2 tablespoons coconut flakes

Direction:

Take a bowl and mix maple syrup, salt, cinnamon, oat flakes, sesame seeds, pumpkin seeds, and coconut flakes. Pour the coconut milk and mix well. Stir in strawberries, mango, and blackberries. Enjoy!

- **Calories:** 373;
- **Total fat:** 11 g;
- **Cholesterol:** 0 mg;
- **Fiber:** 2 g;
- **Protein:** 12 g;
- **Sodium:** 167 mg

7. DELICIOUS SCRAMBLED EGGS

Medium/Gluten-free/Vegetarian Friendly

Preparation time: 10 minutes

Cooking time: 5 minutes

Servings: 2

Ingredients:

- 1 tablespoon peanut oil
- 2 tablespoons nuts, minced
- 4 eggs
- 1 cup shredded broccoli
- 2 tablespoons of Parmesan cheese
- A pinch of salt
- 1 tablespoon fresh parsley, minced

Directions:

Take a bowl and whisk the eggs. Add salt and minced nuts and mix well. Take a skillet and heat on low the peanut oil for 1 minute. Pour the eggs and cook for 2 minutes; then, using a spatula, mix gently the eggs, allowing the uncooked portions to run into the bottom of the skillet. Cook for 3 minutes, mixing gently.

In another bowl, stir the broccoli slaw, a pinch of salt and Parmesan. Mix well. Divide broccoli between 2 plates and top with the eggs. Sprinkle with parsley on each serving. Enjoy!

- **Calories:** 222;
- **Total fat:** 4 g;
- **Fiber:** 2 g;
- **Protein:** 12 g;

8. MEDITERRANEAN SMOOTHIE

| **Preparation Time:** 5 minutes |
| **Cooking Time:** 0 minutes |

- √ 2 cups of spinach
- √ 1 tablespoon fresh ginger root
- √ 1 frozen banana, pre-sliced
- √ 1 small mango, diced
- √ 1/2 cup beet juice
- √ 1/2 cup of skim milk
- √ 6 ice cubes

Servings: 2

Directions:

Take a food processor and put in spinach, frozen banana, small mango, skim milk, fresh ginger root, beet juice and ice cubes. Blend until it is smooth and liquified. Serve cold.

9. FRUIT SMOOTHIE

- √ 2 cups frozen blueberries
- √ 2 cups unsweetened almond milk
- √ 1 teaspoon fresh ground ginger root
- √ 1 frozen banana, pre-sliced
- √ 2 cups frozen raspberries
- √ 6 ice cubes

Preparation Time: 5 minutes
Cooking Time: 0 minutes
Servings: 2

Directions:

Take a food processor and put in blueberries, frozen banana, raspberries, almond milk, fresh ginger root, and ice cubes. Blend until it is smooth and liquified. Serve cold.

10. SWEET KIWI AND MINT SMOOTHIE

- √ 1 cup water, chilled
- √ 2 kiwis, peeled
- √ 1 medium lemon, peeled
- √ ¼ cup mint leaves
- √ ¼ cup parsley leaves
- √ 2 teaspoons honey
- √ 6 ice cubes

Preparation Time: 5 minutes
Cooking Time: 0 minutes
Servings: 1

Directions:

Take a food processor and add water, chopped kiwis, chopped lemon, mint, parsley, honey and ice cubes. Blend for 5 minutes, until well smooth. Serve straight away.

11. OLIVES AND MANGO MIX

- √ 1 cup black olives, pitted and halved
- √ 1 cup Kalamata olives, pitted and halved
- √ 1 cup mango, peeled and cubed
- √ A pinch of salt and black pepper
- √ Juice of 1 lime
- √ 1 teaspoon sweet paprika
- √ 1 teaspoon coriander, ground
- √ 1 tablespoon olive oil

Preparation Time: 10 minutes
Cooking Time: 0 minutes
Servings: 2

Directions
1. In a bowl mix the olives with the mango and olive oil. Mix well.
2. Add paprika, coriander, lemon juice, salt and pepper. Mix and serve.

12. <u>TEA WITH COCONUT</u>

√ 2 tea bags, cinnamon-flavored

√ ¼ cup coconut milk, unsweetened

√ 2 cups building water

Preparation Time: 10 minutes
Cooking Time: 0 minutes
Servings: 2

Directions
1. Pour boiling water between two mugs, add a tea into each mug and let them steep for 5 minutes.
2. Meanwhile, take a small saucepan, place it over medium heat, pour in coconut milk and heat for 3 minutes.
3. After 5 minutes, remove tea bags from mugs, stir in milk until combined and serve!

13. <u>RASPBERRY ICE CREAM</u>

√ 2 cup frozen raspberries

√ ½ cup almond milk

√ ½ cup heavy cream

√ ¼ teaspoon stevia powder

Preparation Time: 6 hours 5 minutes
Cooking Time: 0 minutes
Servings: 2

Directions
1. Take a food processor and combine raspberries, heavy cream, almond milk and stevia. Blend for 5 minutes until smooth. Pour the batter in 2 ice cream ramekins and chill for at least 6 hours. Enjoy!

14. <u>GINGER COOKIES</u>

√ 2 cups of flour

√ ¾ cup granulated sugar

√ 2 teaspoons ginger powder

Servings: 4
Preparation Time: 30 minutes
Cooking Time: 12 minutes

- √ 1 teaspoon cinnamon
- √ ½ teaspoon nutmeg
- √ ¼ teaspoon salt
- √ 1 egg
- √ 1 teaspoon vanilla extract

Directions

Preheat the oven to 350°F. Take a baking dish with parchment paper. In a bowl whisk egg, flour, sugar and ginger powder. Add cinnamon, nutmeg, salt and vanilla extract. Stir until the batter is smooth. Using a spoon, pour a bit of batter on the prepared baking sheets to form biscuits. Bake for 10 minutes. Let them rest 10 minutes before serving.

15. **PINA COLADA BARS**

CRUST:
- √ 1 cup almond meal
- √ 2 tablespoons coconut oil
- √ 1 tablespoon water
- √ 1 tablespoon canola oil
- √ 2 tablespoons sugar
- √ 2 tablespoons coconut flour
- √ ½ teaspoon ground ginger

FILLING:
- √ ½ cup of white sugar
- √ 1 cup cottage cheese
- √ 1 ½ tablespoon lemon zest
- √ ¼ cup cream cheese
- √ 1 tablespoon pineapple juice
- √ ½ teaspoon vanilla extract

Prep Time: 35 minutes	
Cooking Time: 35 minutes	
Servings: 10	

TOPPING:
- √ 1 cup of chopped pineapple
- √ ¼ cup unsweetened coconut flakes

- √ 1 egg
- √ Salt to taste

Directions

1. Preheat the oven 325°F. Take a baking pan with parchment paper.

Take a bowl and combine almond meal, coconut oil, water, canola oil and coconut flour. Mix well. Add sugar and ground ginger. Mix well until it is uniform. Pour the mixture into the bottom of baking pan and bake it for 10 minutes.

To make the filling, blend all the filling ingredients in a food processor. Once the crust is ready, spread the filling mixture over the cooled crust and bake it for 35 minutes. Cool down for 20 minutes, until completely chilled. Top with chopped coconut and pineapple and serve!

16. **PEANUT BUTTER BANANA PUDDING**

√   2 bananas, halved
√   ¼ cup smooth peanut butter
√   ½ cup of coconut flakes for garnish

Directions

Take a food processor and add bananas and peanut butter.

Blend for 5-6 minutes, until smooth or desired texture obtained.

Pour into a bowl and garnish with coconut flakes.

Enjoy!

| **Prep Time:** 15 minutes |
| **Cooking Time:** 25 minutes |
| **Servings:** 2 |

17. VANILLA AVOCADO POPSICLES

Preparation Time: 20 minutes   **Cooking Time:** 0 minutes   **Servings:** 4

Ingredients:

- 2 avocadoes, peeled
- 1 teaspoon vanilla extract
- 1 cup almond milk
- 1 teaspoon stevia liquid
- ½ cup cocoa powder

Directions: In a blender add all the listed ingredients and blend until smooth. Pour blended mixture into the Popsicle molds and place in the freezer for at least 4 hours. Serve and enjoy!

18. CHOCOLATE POPSICLE

Preparation Time: 4 hours 10 minutes

Cooking Time: 10 minutes

Servings: 4

Ingredients:

- 4 cups chocolate, chopped
- 6 teaspoons stevia liquid
- 2 cups heavy cream

Directions:

Add heavy cream into a pot and heat on low until boil. Stir the chocolate into the heavy cream and whisk to combine. Add liquid stevia into the cream mixture and stir for at least 5 minutes, until chocolate is melted. Pour mixture into the Popsicle molds and place in freezer for 4 hours. Serve and enjoy.

CHAPTER 2. LUNCH

19. AWESOME MEDITERRANEAN OMELET

Easy/Gluten-free
Preparation time: 5 minutes
Cooking time: 32 minutes
Servings: 4
Ingredients:

- 1 tablespoon pepper
- ½ cup sun-dried tomatoes
- 2 cups of spinaches
- ½ tablespoon zaatar spices
- 6 eggs, beaten
- ½ cup Feta cheese
- 2 tablespoons olive oil
- 1 can of peas, drained
- 1 zucchini, sliced
- Salt and pepper to taste

Directions:

Preheat the oven to 325°F. Take a baking dish with parchment paper.

Take a skillet and heat on low the olive oil. Add the peas, and cook for 10 minutes, often stirring. Add the sun-dried tomatoes, spinach, spices, and zucchini, and saute for 5 minutes until the spinach is crushed. Once spinaches are ready, pour the vegetable mixture in the baking dish; then pour the beaten eggs to cover the mix. Add a pinch of salt and pepper. Bake for 8 minutes. Add the Feta cheese, crumbled, and season with salt and pepper. Bake the frittata for another 10 minutes. Serve immediately.

Nutrition:

- **Calories:** 311;
- **Total fat:** 4 g;
- **Cholesterol:** 84 mg;
- **Fiber**: 2 g;
- **Protein:** 12 g;
- **Sodium:** 357 mg

20. DELICIOUS BASIL LEMON RATATOUILLE

√ 1 eggplant, cut into cubes
√ 5 leaves of fresh basil
√ 2 cups cherry tomatoes, chopped
√ 1 onion, chopped
√ 2 summer squash, sliced
√ 2 zucchinis, sliced
√ 2 tablespoons vinegar
√ 1 tablespoon tomato paste
√ 2 garlic cloves, minced

Preparation Time: 35 minutes	
Cooking Time: 30 minutes	
Servings: 4	

√ 3 tablespoons olive oil
√ Salt to taste
√ 1 cup of water
√ 1 fresh lemon juice

Directions

1. Take your food processor. Add basil, vinegar, tomato paste, garlic, lemon juice, oil, and salt into the blender and blend until smooth.

2. Take a non-stick pot and heat olive oil on medium. Add onion and cook for 3-4 minutes. Add to pot eggplant, tomatoes, squash, water, and zucchini. Cook for 15 minutes, occasionally stirring.

4. Pour blended basil mixture into the pot and stir well. Continue to cook for 10 minutes, seasoning with salt. Once done, let it rest for 20 minutes, allow to heat pressure naturally. Stir well and serve.

21. MEDITERRANEAN PASTA SALAD

- √ 3 ounces of Pasta
- √ 1 cup Fresh Lettuce
- √ 2 large tomatoes, sliced
- √ ½ cup of Feta cheese, crumbled
- √ ½ red bell pepper, sliced
- √ 1 carrot, sliced
- √ 1 cucumber, sliced
- √ Salt and pepper to taste
- √ 2 tablespoons of extra virgin olive oil
- √ ½ tablespoon oregano

Preparation Time: 10 minutes
Cooking Time: 10 minutes
Servings: 2

Directions

1. Take a pot and bring the water to a boil. Season with salt and add Pasta. Cook on low for 10 minutes.

2. Meanwhile, take a bowl and add tomatoes red bell pepper, carrot, olive oil, oregano and cucumber and mix well. Chop lettuce and add to the bowl. Mix.

3. Once Pasta is cooked, drain it and place it in the vegetable mix. Enjoy!

22. RICE AND VEGGIES SALAD

- √ 1 cup of rice
- √ 2 eggs
- √ 2 tablespoons of capers
- √ 2 large tomatoes, sliced
- √ ½ cup of Feta Cheese
- √ 2 tablespoons of olive oil
- √ Salt and pepper to taste
- √ 1 teaspoon oregano

Preparation Time: 15 minutes
Cooking Time: 20 minutes
Servings: 2

Directions

1. Take a pot and bring the water to a boil. Season with salt, add rice and cook for 18 minutes.

2. Meanwhile, take a little pot and add in the water. Place the eggs and cook for 15 minutes on low. Once they are cooked, drain, shell and chop the eggs.

3. In a bowl, combine tomatoes, olive oil and oregano and mix well. Add feta cheese, capers, eggs and rice. Mix well and serve.

23. MEDITERRANEAN POTATO SALAD

√	3 tablespoons extra virgin olive oil	**Preparation Time:** 30 minutes
√	½ cup black olives, sliced	**Cooking Time:** 20 minutes
√	3 tablespoons lemon juice	**Servings:** 6
√	2 tablespoons of mint, chopped	
√	Salt and pepper to taste	
√	½ celery stalk, sliced	
√	2 pounds potatoes	
√	2 tablespoons of chopped oregano	
√	Water	

Directions

1. Cut the potatoes into inch cubes. Toss the potatoes into a medium skillet and cover them with water. Cook on medium-high for 5 minutes, until the water starts boiling. Then, reduce the heat to medium-low, season with 1 ½ teaspoons of salt and simmer the potatoes for 15 minutes.
2. Meanwhile, take a bowl and mix the olive oil, lemon juice, and a pinch of salt and pepper. Whisk well.
3. Drain the potatoes, pour them into a bowl and mix well. Stir in the celery stalk and olives. Sprinkle with the mint and oregano. Mix and serve!

24. BROCCOLI, ASPARAGUS AND CHEESE FRITTATA

Preparation Time: 10 minutes	
Cooking Time: 26 minutes	
Servings: 2	

√ ½ cup of Feta cheese
√ ¼ cup chopped broccoli florets
√ 1-ounce asparagus spears cutted
√ ½ garlic clove, minced
√ 2 tablespoons whipping cream
√ 2 eggs
√ 2 tablespoons avocado oil
√ A pinch of salt

√ A pinch of black pepper

Directions: Preheat the oven to 350° F.

Take a medium bowl, crack eggs in it, add salt, black pepper and cream, whisk until combined and then stir in cheese. Let it rest for 5-6 minutes. Take a medium skillet and heat avocado oil on medium. Add garlic and saute for 2 minutes, often stirring. Add broccoli florets and asparagus and cook for 10 minutes, stirring. Spread the vegetables evenly in the pan, pour egg mixture over them and cook for 1 to 2 minutes until the mixture begins. Transfer the pan into the oven and then cook for 10 to 12 minutes until frittata has cooked and the top has turned golden brown. Cut the frittata into slices and serve.

25. GARLIC ZUCCHINI AND CAULIFLOWER

Preparation Time: 10 minutes
Cooking Time: 20 minutes
Servings: 4
Ingredients:

- 4 zucchinis, cut into medium fries
- 1 cup cauliflower florets

- 1 tablespoon capers, drained
- Juice of ½ lemon
- A pinch of salt and black pepper
- ½ teaspoon chili powder
- 1 tablespoon olive oil
- ¼ teaspoon garlic powder

Directions:

Spread the zucchini fries on a lined baking sheet, add the rest of the ingredients, toss, introduce in the oven, bake at 400°F for 20 minutes, divide between plates and serve.

26. MARINARA BROCCOLI

Preparation Time: 10 minutes
Cooking Time: 15 minutes
Servings: 4
Ingredients:

- 2 cups broccoli florets
- 1 teaspoon sweet paprika
- 1 tablespoon coriander, minced

- ¼ cup marinara sauce
- A pinch of salt and pepper
- ½ teaspoon chili powder
- 1 tablespoon olive oil
- ½ teaspoon garlic powder
- Juice of 1 lime

Directions:

In a roasting pan, mix the broccoli with the marinara and the other ingredients, toss and bake at 400 degrees F for 15 minutes. Divide between plates and serve.

27. BEANS AND CHICKPEAS SALAD

Preparation Time: 30 minutes
Cooking Time: 15 minutes
Servings: 2
Ingredients:

- ½ cup dry black beans
- ½ cup dry chickpeas

- ½ onion, diced
- 1 red bell pepper, seeded, sliced
- 2 cups spinach, fresh or frozen, chopped
- 4 cherry tomatoes, chopped
- 1 avocado, peeled, cubed

- ½ teaspoon chili powder
- ½ teaspoon cumin
- Salt and pepper to taste
- 2 tablespoons extra-virgin olive oil
- 1 tablespoon balsamic vinegar

Directions:

Take a pot and bring the water to a boil. Season with salt and add beans and chickpeas. Cook on medium for 15 minutes. Put all of the ingredients into a large bowl. Toss the mix of veggies and spices until combined thoroughly.

Store, or serve chilled with some olive oil and vinegar on top!

28. LETTUCE MIX SALAD

Easy/Gluten-free/Vegan
Preparation time: 5 minutes
Cooking time: 0 minutes
Servings: 4

Ingredients:

- 2 tablespoons extra-virgin olive oil
- A pinch of salt and pepper
- 1 red onion, sliced
- Juice of 1 lime
- 5 basil leaves, minced
- 2 cups romaine lettuce, chopped
- 1 cup radicchios, chopped

- 2 tomatoes, chopped

Directions:

Take a bowl, and mix chopped tomatoes, olive oil, minced basil leaves, and a pinch of salt and pepper. Stir in the lettuce, onion and radicchios. Drizzle with lemon juice and serve!

- **Fats:** 2 g,
- **Fiber:** 1 g,
- **Carbs:** 1 g,
- **Protein:** 2 g

29. PARMESAN ZUCCHINI ROUNDS

Vegetarian Friendly
Preparation Time: 25 minutes
Cooking Time: 20 minutes
Servings: 4
Ingredients:

- 4 zucchinis, sliced
- 2 cups parmesan, grated
- ¼ cup parsley, chopped.
- 1 egg, whisked
- 1 egg white, whisked
- ½ teaspoon garlic powder
- 2 tablespoons olive oil
- A pinch of salt and pepper

Directions:

Preheat the oven to 370°F. Take a baking dish with parchment paper.

Take a bowl and mix the egg with egg whites, and a pinch of salt and pepper. Add parmesan, parsley, olive oil, and garlic powder and whisk well. Stir in the zucchinis and mix well. Place zucchini mix into the baking dish and bake for 20 minutes. Serve warm!

30. CRUCIFEROUS SALAD

Easy/Gluten-free
Preparation time: 15 minutes
Cooking time: 0 minutes
Servings: 4
Ingredients:

- 1 cup green kale
- 10 Brussels sprouts
- 1 cup shredded green cabbage
- 1 tablespoon extra-virgin olive oil
- 2 tablespoons almonds
- ½ cup shredded Parmesan cheese
- 2 tablespoons lemon juice
- 1 garlic clove, finely minced
- Salt and pepper to taste

Directions:

1. Wash and dry the kale, Brussels sprouts, and cabbage and chop them. Put the chopped cruciferous in a bowl and pour the olive oil. Mix well and add almonds, olive oil, minced garlic clove, Parmesan, salt and pepper. Drizzle with lemon juice and mix well. Serve!

Nutrition:

- **Calories:** 440;
- **Total fat:** 32 g;
- **Cholesterol:** 35 mg;
- **Protein:** 14 g;
- **Sodium:** 427 mg

CHAPTER 3. DINNERS

31. KIDNEY BEAN AND POMEGRANATE SALAD

Preparation Time: 10 minutes

Cooking Time: 0 minutes

Servings: 3

Ingredients:

- 2 cans white kidney beans, drained
- 1 cup fresh pomegranate seeds
- ½ red onion, chopped
- 2 tablespoons parsley, chopped
- 1 tablespoon lime juice
- Salt and pepper to taste

Directions:

1. In a large serving bowl, place all the ingredients and toss to coat well. Serve immediately.

32. SPINACH AND ORANGE SALAD

Preparation Time: 15 minutes

Cooking Time: 0 minutes

Servings: 4

Ingredients:

- 2 tablespoons mustard
- 3 oranges, peeled
- 3 cups spinach, torn
- 1 red onion, chopped

Directions:

Take a bowl and stir in sliced onion, chopped orange wedges and chopped spinaches. Mix and add mustard. Serve!

33. RED PEPPER AND BROCCOLI SALAD

Preparation Time: 15 minutes

Cooking Time: 0 minutes

Servings: 2

Ingredients:

- 2 cups lettuce romaine, chopped
- 1 cup broccoli, chopped
- ½ red bell pepper, seeded

DRESSING:

- 3 tablespoons wine vinegar
- 1 teaspoon mustard
- 1 garlic clove, peeled
- Salt and pepper to taste
- 2 tablespoons olive oil
- 1 tablespoon parsley, minced

Directions:

1. Take a pot and bring the water to a boil. Season with salt and cook broccoli for 10 minutes. Drain them.
2. Take a bowl, add broccoli, chopped lettuce and chopped bell pepper. Add wine vinegar, mustard, garlic sliced, olive oil, parsley, a pinch of salt and pepper. Mix well and serve!

34. LENTIL POTATO SALAD

Preparation Time: 35 minutes

Cooking Time: 25 minutes

Servings: 2

Ingredients:

- ½ cup beluga lentils
- 2 potatoes, peeled
- ½ onion, sliced

Directions:

1. Bring two cups of water to simmer in a pot and add your lentils. Cook for 20 minutes, then drain only the lentils.
2. Reduce the heat on low and add potatoes into the water from before.

35. <u>MINI ZUCCHINIS CUP</u>

Easy
Preparation Time: 5 Minutes
Cooking Time: 20 Minutes
Servings: 4
Ingredients:

- 4 Zucchinis, cubed

Direction:

- 4 cherry tomatoes
- 2 tablespoons lemon juice
- Salt and pepper to taste
  Cook potatoes for 15 minutes, then drain and chop them.

3. Put your lentils on a serving plate. Top with onion, chopped potatoes and chopped tomatoes. Season with a pinch of salt and pepper, drizzle with the lemon juice and serve!

- ½ cup Mozzarella cheese, cubed
- 1-layer Pizza dough
- ½ cup black olives
- Olive oil to grease
- ½ cup of Parmesan cheese

Preheat the oven to 375°. Take a muffin pan and lightly grease each cup with olive oil. Place the dough in each pan's cup, removing the excess. Place cubed zucchini into each cup. Top with cubed Mozzarella cheese and sliced olives. Sprinkle Parmesan cheese on top. Bake for 20 minutes. Serve warm!

- **Calories:** 50
- **Fats:** 3 g

- **Carbs:** 3 g
- **Protein:** 3 g

CHAPTER 4. DESSERTS

36. PEACH ICE POPS

Easy/Gluten-free/Dairy-Free
Preparation time: 6 hours
Cooking time: 0 minutes
Servings: 6
Ingredients:

- 1 can light coconut milk
- 2 peaches, peeled, chopped
- 3 tablespoons honey
- A pinch of cinnamon

Directions:
Take a food processor and add the coconut milk, peaches, honey, and cinnamon. Blend until smooth.
Pour the mixture into ice pop molds and freeze for 6 hours. Serve with your favorite garnish!
Nutrition:

- **Calories:** 79;
- **Total fat:** 3 g;
- **Cholesterol:** 0 mg;
- **Fiber:** 2 g;
- **Protein:** 0 g;
- **Sodium:** 4 mg

37. MINT & LIME SORBET

Easy/Gluten-free/Dairy-free
Preparation time: 1 hours
Cooking time: 0 minutes
Servings: 6
Ingredients:

- 2 cups mint, fresh
- 2 lime, peeled
- 2 tablespoons honey
- 2 tablespoons lime juice
- A pinch of cinnamon
- Water as needed
- 1 teaspoon stevia liquid

Directions:
Take a food processor, add chopped mint, chopped lime wedges, the honey, lime juice, stevia, and cinnamon.
Blend until smooth, adding water if needed to purée the sorbet.
Transfer the mixture to a container and freeze for at least 1 hour.

- **Calories:** 97;
- **Total fat:** 0 g;
- **Cholesterol:** 0 mg;
- **Fiber:** 2 g;
- **Protein:** 2 g;
- **Sodium:** 39 mg

38. MANDARIN CREAM

Easy/Gluten-free
Preparation time: 3 hours to freeze

Cooking time: 5 minutes
Servings: 6

Ingredients:

- ½ cup coconut cream, frozen overnight
- 1 cup coconut, shredded
- 3 small mandarins, peeled
- ½ cup sour cream

Directions:

In a large bowl, beat the cold coconut cream until it forms stiff peaks. Stir in coconut, mandarins' segments, and sour cream until well mixed. Cover and chill in the refrigerator for 3 hours before serving.

- **Calories:** 281;
- **Total fat:** 22 g;
- **Cholesterol:** 4 mg;
- **Fiber:** 2 g;
- **Protein:** 6 g;
- **Sodium:** 31 mg

39. CHOCOLATE-QUINOA PUDDING

Easy/Gluten-free
Preparation time: 5 minutes
Cooking time: 20 minutes
Servings: 6
Ingredients:

- 2 cups almond milk
- 2 cups quinoa
- 1 cup coconut milk
- ½ cup cocoa powder
- A pinch of salt
- 1 teaspoon vanilla extract

Directions:

Take a skillet and heat on low the almond milk, quinoa, coconut milk, cocoa powder, salt, and vanilla.

Bring the quinoa mixture to a boil and then reduce the heat to low. Simmer for 20 minutes, until the quinoa is tender, stirring frequently. Remove the pudding from the heat. Serve warm in a bowl!

- **Calories:** 241;
- **Total fat:** 6 g;
- **Cholesterol:** 0 mg;
- **Fiber:** 2 g;
- **Protein:** 6 g;
- **Sodium:** 161 mg

40. PEARS WITH HAZELNUTS

Easy/Gluten-free
Preparation time: 15 minutes
Cooking time: 10 minutes
Servings: 2
Ingredients:

- 1 tablespoon butter
- 2 pears, cored and chopped
- ½ cup of water
- 2 tablespoons goat cheese
- 2 tablespoons honey
- ½ cup hazelnuts, chopped

Directions:

Preheat the oven to 350°F. Take a baking dish with parchment paper.

Take a skillet and melt the butter on medium. Add the pears and lightly brown them, for 2 minutes.

Place the pears in the baking dish. Pour the water into the baking dish, taking care not to get any in the hollow part of the pears. Roast the pears for 10 minutes. Remove the pears from the oven.

Take a bowl, stir in the goat cheese, honey, and hazelnuts. Add pears and serve warm!

- **Calories:** 185;

- **Total fat:** 9 g;
- **Cholesterol:** 15 mg;
- **Fiber:** 2 g;
- **Protein:** 4 g;
- **Sodium:** 17 mg

41. PANNA COTTA WITH MANGO

Easy/Gluten-free
Preparation time: 3 hours 10 minutes
Cooking time: 2 minutes
Servings: 4
Ingredients:

- ½ cup coconut milk
- 2 teaspoons agar-agar
- 2 cups buttermilk
- 2 tablespoons honey
- 2 cups fresh mango, chopped

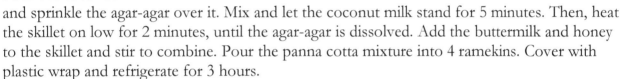

Directions:
Pour the coconut milk into a skillet and sprinkle the agar-agar over it. Mix and let the coconut milk stand for 5 minutes. Then, heat the skillet on low for 2 minutes, until the agar-agar is dissolved. Add the buttermilk and honey to the skillet and stir to combine. Pour the panna cotta mixture into 4 ramekins. Cover with plastic wrap and refrigerate for 3 hours.
Top with mango and serve.

- **Calories:** 226;
- **Total fat:** 8 g;
- **Cholesterol:** 14 mg;
- **Fiber:** 2 g;
- **Protein:** 6 g;
- **Sodium:** 106 mg

42. CINANMON SWEET POTATOES

Easy/Gluten-free
Preparation time: 3 hours 15 minutes
Cooking time: 15 minutes
Servings: 4
Ingredients:

- 2 sweet potatoes, peeled, chopped
- 1 cup coconut cream, chilled overnight
- 2 tablespoons maple syrup
- ½ teaspoon cinnamon
- A pinch of salt
- ½ cup hazelnuts, minced

Directions:
Place the sweet potatoes in a pot and fill with water until the sweet potatoes are covered. Bring to a boil and cook for 15 minutes. Drain and mash with a potato masher or a fork, until smooth. Transfer the sweet potatoes to a container and let them set it in the fridge for 2 hours.
Take a bowl, whisk the cold coconut cream until stiff peaks form.

In another bowl, stir together the sweet potatoes, maple syrup, cinnamon, and salt. Add coconut cream and mix keeping as much volume as possible. Chill the sweet potato mix in the fridge for 1 hour.

Spoon the sweet potato mixture into 4 bowls, top with hazelnuts and serve!

- **Calories:** 281;
- **Cholesterol:** 0 mg;
- **Protein:** 2 g;
- **Total fat:** 12 g;
- **Fiber:** 2 g;
- **Sodium:** 70 mg

43. DARK CHOCOLATE CAKE

Easy/Gluten-free
Preparation time: 12 hours
Cooking time: 45 minutes
Servings: 6

Ingredients:

- ½ cup of water
- 1 cup granulated sugar
- A pinch of salt
- ½ pounds 60% cacao chocolate, chopped
- ½ cup salted butter, cubed
- 4 eggs
- 1 teaspoon pure vanilla extract

Directions:

Preheat the oven to 300°F. Grease a 9-inch round springform pan and set the pan on a piece of foil. Fold the foil up the outside of the pan, forming a waterproof layer. Set aside.

Take a pot and heat on medium the water. Add the sugar and salt, stirring until the sugar is completely dissolved. Remove the pot from the heat and set aside. Place the chocolate in a large bowl over a medium pot full of simmering water and melt the chocolate, stirring gently. Once melted, stir in the butter (one cube at a time) and mix well to combine. Remove the chocolate from the heat. Pour the chocolate in the sugar mixture and mix well to combine. Add the eggs (one at a time), constantly stirring. Add the vanilla and whisk until smooth.

Pour the batter into the prepared springform pan and place the pan into a larger pan. Pour boiling water into the larger pan until it reaches one inch up the sides of the springform pan. Bake the cake for 45 minutes. Remove the cake from the oven. Let cool down and chill the cake in the refrigerator overnight. Remove from the springform pan when ready to serve.

44. CREPES WITH BLUEBERRY AND COCONUT CREAM

Ingredients:
CREPE BATTER:
- √ 1½ cups almond milk
- √ 2 eggs
- √ 1½ tablespoons honey
- √ 1 tablespoon coconut oil

Dairy-free
Preparation Time: 15 minutes
Cooking Time: 20 minutes
Servings: 5
Difficulty: Medium

- √ ¼ teaspoon salt
- √ 1 cup almond flour

BLUEBERRY SAUCE:
- √ 1 cup blueberries
- √ 1 tablespoon lemon juice
- √ 1 tsp honey

COCONUT WHIPPED CREAM:
- √ 1 can coconut milk
- √ 2 teaspoons honey
- √ ¼ teaspoon cinnamon

Directions:

In a bowl or container, mix all crepe batter ingredients until smooth. Chill in the refrigerator. For the coconut cream, using an electric hand mixer, blend all ingredients until peaks begin to form

Blueberry sauce: Put all ingredients in a food processor and process until the sauce is completely smooth. To make the crepes, heat a small nonstick skillet. The pan must be greased with a nonstick cooking spray and scoop the batter to the center of the pan. To spread the batter out thin and evenly, swirl the pan. Cook the crepe for 30 seconds, then gently flip it and cook the other side for 10–15 seconds. Serve the crepes rolled, topped with the blueberry sauce, and a dollop of the cinnamon-coconut whipped cream.

45. GLUTEN-FREE CHOCOLATE CAKE

Dairy-free

Preparation Time: 20 minutes
Cooking Time: 25 minutes
Servings: 8
Difficulty: Medium

- √ ½ cup rice flour
- √ ¼ cup sorghum flour
- √ ¼ cup almond flour
- √ ½ cup tapioca starch
- √ ¼ cup potato starch
- √ ½ tsp. gelatin
- √ ¼ tsp. salt
- √ 1½ tsp. baking powder
- √ 1 tsp. baking soda
- √ 1½ cups sugar
- √ 4 eggs
- √ 2 tsp. vanilla extract
- √ 1 cup sour cream
- √ 1 cup of coconut oil
- √ ¾ cup chocolate chips
- √ ½ cup cacao powder

Directions: Oven: 350°F

Cream together sugar, eggs, and vanilla. After it is well combined, add the sour cream. Add the dry ingredients to the wet mixture. Set aside. In a heated saucepan, the butter, coconut oil & chocolate chips must be melted. Whisk in cocoa powder. Add the chocolate mixture to the other bowl. Pour cake batter into two 9" cake pans. Bake for 25–27 minutes.

CHAPTER 5. SPECIAL RECIPES

46. GARLIC CAULIFLOWER

Easy/Dairy-free/Vegan/Gluten-free
Preparation Time: 10 minutes
Cooking time: 13 minutes
Servings: 2
Ingredients:

- 2 cups cauliflower
- 2 tablespoons olive oil
- 3 garlic cloves, minced
- Salt and pepper to taste
- 1 tablespoon lemon juice
- ½ teaspoon lemon zest
- 2 tablespoons chives, minced

Directions:

Take a skillet and heat the olive oil on medium. Add minced garlic cloves and cook for 2 minutes, stirring. Add chopped cauliflower and cook for 5 minutes, often stirring. Season with salt and pepper, then add lemon zest and chives and cook for another 8 minutes. Remove from the heat, drizzle with lemon juice and serve!

- **Calories:** 178
- **Carbohydrate:** 14 g
- **Cholesterol:** 18 mg
- **Total Fat:** 18 g
- **Fiber:** 4 g
- **Protein:** 2 g

47. CHEESE BEETS

Easy/Gluten-free
Preparation Time: 15 minutes
Cooking time: 15 minutes
Servings: 2
Ingredients:

- 2 cups beet tops, chopped
- 1 tablespoon olive oil
- 1 tablespoon balsamic vinegar
- 2 cups goat cheese, goat cheese
- Salt to taste
- 1 tablespoon dill, minced
- 2 tablespoons walnuts, minced

Directions:

Take a skillet and heat the olive oil on medium. Add the beets and cook for 5 minutes. Stir in the goat cheese and dill and cook for 10 minutes, constantly stirring to avoid cheese lumps. Season with salt. Transfer the beets into a bowl, pour the balsamic vinegar, garnish with minced walnuts and serve!

- **Calories:** 215
- **Cholesterol:** 12 mg
- **Fiber: 2 g**
- **Carbohydrate:** 4 g
- **Total Fat:** 18 g
- **Protein:** 10 g

48. SPICY CAULIFLOWER

Easy/Dairy-free/Vegan
Preparation Time: 25 minutes
Cooking time: 20 minutes
Servings: 4
Ingredients:

- 2 cups cauliflower
- 1 celery stalk, sliced
- 2 tablespoons olive oil
- 2 rosemary sprigs
- 1 tablespoon thyme, chopped
- 1 tablespoon paprika

- 1 teaspoon cumin
- Salt and pepper to taste
- 2 tablespoons lemon juice

Directions:

Take a skillet and heat the olive oil on medium. Add sliced celery stalk and saute for 3 minutes, often stirring. Add the cauliflower and stir for 1 minute to combine. Season with salt and pepper and add paprika, thyme, cumin, and rosemary sprigs and cook for 15 minutes, often stirring. Drizzle with lemon juice and serve!

- **Calories:** 225
- **Carbohydrate:** 4 g
- **Cholesterol:** 1 mg
- **Total Fat:** 20 g
- **Fiber:** 0 g
- **Protein:** 5 g

49. CHEDDAR SPICY BISCUITS

Easy/Gluten-free
Preparation Time: 20 minutes
Cooking time: 15 minutes
Servings: 6
Ingredients:

- ½ cup coconut oil
- 4 eggs
- 2 teaspoon apple vinegar
- 2 cup almond flour
- ½ teaspoon baking powder
- A pinch of salt
- 1 cup cheddar cheese, melted
- 1 teaspoon cinnamon
- 1 small jalapenos, minced

Preheat the oven to 400°F. Take a baking dish with parchment paper.

Take a bowl and whisk the eggs. Season with a pinch of salt and stir in the coconut oil, melted cheese, and apple vinegar. Mix well to combine. Take another bowl and mix almond flour, cinnamon, baking powder and minced jalapenos. Stir to combine. Pour the eggs batter into the flour mixture, little by little, constantly mixing to avoid lumps. Stir until uniform. Work with your hands to form 10-12 small balls with the dough. Make to the dough the form you want and place the biscuits onto the parchment paper. Bake for 15 minutes, until golden brown. Serve!

- **Calories:** 260
- **Carbohydrate:** 4 g
- **Cholesterol:** 8 mg
- **Total Fat:** 22 g
- **Fiber:** 1 g
- **Protein:** 4 g

50. FRESH ROASTED RADISH

Easy/Gluten-free
Preparation Time: 15 minutes
Cooking time: 13 minutes
Servings: 4
Ingredients:

- 1 tablespoon coconut oil
- 1 cup radishes, chopped
- Salt and pepper to taste
- 2 teaspoons chives, minced
- 1 rosemary sprig
- 1 teaspoon thyme, minced
- 1 teaspoon fresh mint, minced

Directions:

Remove the tops and stems from the radishes. Take a cast iron pan and heat coconut oil on medium. Add chopped radishes and saute for 3 minutes. Season with salt and pepper and cook for 5 minutes, often stirring. Add chives, rosemary sprig, thyme and mint and cook for another 5 minutes, often stirring. Serve!

- **Calories:** 123
- **Cholesterol:** 8 mg
- **Carbohydrate:** 6 g

51. DELICIOUS MEDITERRANEAN "BRUSCHETTA"

Easy/Dairy-free/Vegetarian Friendly
Preparation Time: 15 min
Cooking Time: 10 minutes
Servings: 4

- 4 basil leaves, minced
- 2 tablespoons black olives, sliced
- 2 tablespoons capers
- 4 tomatoes, finely chopped
- 1 tablespoon balsamic vinegar
- 2 tablespoons extra-virgin olive oil
- ½ red onion, finely chopped
- Salt and pepper to taste
- 1 tablespoon oregano, minced
- 1 garlic clove, finely minced
- 4 slices of whole bread

Directions:

Preheat the oven to 375°F. Take a baking dish with parchment paper.

Place the slices of bread into the baking dish and toast into the oven for 3 minutes per side. Meanwhile, take a bowl and mix finely chopped tomatoes with olive oil, minced basil leaves, oregano and a pinch of salt and pepper. Add capers, garlic clove, onion, and finely sliced olives. Pour balsamic vinegar and toss to combine. Place the tomatoes mix on each slice of bread and serve!

- **Calories:** 152
- **Carbohydrate:** 4 g
- **Cholesterol:** 1 mg
- **Total Fat:** 13 g
- **Protein:** 1 g
- **Sodium:** 140 mg

52. TOMATO CHEESE SOUP

Easy/Vegetarian Friendly
Preparation time: 25 minutes
Cooking time: 20 minutes
Serving: 3

- 1 garlic clove, minced
- 2 cans tomato sauce
- 1 cup white wine
- 2 tablespoons butter, cubed
- 4 basil leaves, minced
- Salt and pepper to taste
- 2 cups cheddar cheese, shredded
- 1 teaspoon white sugar
- 1 cup cubed toast bread

Directions:

Take a pot and heat tomato sauce on medium. Add minced garlic clove, minced basil leaves, and white sugar. Mix well and cook for 5 minutes. Add cheddar cheese, butter, and a pinch of salt and pepper and cook for another 5 minutes, constantly stirring to melt the cheese. Increase the heat on medium-high and pour the wine. Cook for 5-6 minutes, stirring until the whine is evaporated. Reduce the heat and cook for another 2 minutes on medium. Place the cubed bread into the soup and enjoy!

- **Calories:** 118
- **Carbohydrate:** 4 g
- **Cholesterol:** 30 mg
- **Total Fat:** 10 g
- **Fiber:** 1 g
- **Protein**: 4 g

53. CHEESE SEAFOOD

Medium

Preparation time: 25 minutes

Cooking time: 20 minutes
Servings: 4
Ingredients:
- 2 tablespoons olive oil
- 2 garlic cloves
- 1 cup shrimp, drained
- 1 cup crabmeat, thawed

- ½ cup Parmesan cheese, shredded
- ½ cup Ricotta cheese
- 2 eggs
- ½ celery stalk, chopped
- ½ onion, chopped
- 2 tablespoons parsley, chopped
- Salt and pepper to taste

Directions:
Take skillet and heat the olive oil on medium. Add garlic cloves and saute for 2 minutes, stirring. Add shrimp and crabmeat and cook for 10 minutes, frequently stirring.
Meanwhile, take a food processor and mix Parmesan, parsley, onion, and celery stalk. Blend for 3 minutes. Take a bowl and beat the eggs. Stir in Ricotta cheese and whisk well with the eggs. Add the Parmesan mixture and stir to combine. Season with salt and pepper. Pour the cheese mixture into the skillet and stir with crabmeat and shrimps. Cook for 8 minutes, constantly stirring. Serve warm.

- **Calories:** 57
- **Carbohydrate:** 5 g

- **Cholesterol:** 22 mg
- **Total Fat:** 3 g

- **Fiber:** 1 g
- **Protein:** 3 g

54. DELICIOUS VEGGIE MIX

Medium/Gluten-free/Vegetarian friendly
Preparation Time: 25 minutes
Cooking Time: 20 minutes
Servings: 2
- 2 Zucchinis, chopped
- 1 cup pumpkin, peeled and chopped

- Salt and pepper to taste
- 2 potatoes, peeled and chopped
- 1 teaspoon thyme, minced
- 1 teaspoon mint, minced
- 1 garlic clove, minced
- 2 tablespoons butter
- ½ cup Parmesan cheese, grated

Directions:
Take a skillet and melt the butter on low. Add garlic clove and saute for 2 minutes until fragrant, often stirring. Increase the heat on medium and add chopped pumpkin and chopped potatoes and cook for 10 minutes, often stirring. Add chopped zucchinis and cook for 3 minutes, often stirring. Season with salt and pepper and add thyme and mint. Cook for another 5 minutes, often stirring. Sprinkle with Parmesan and serve!

- **Calories:** 122
- **Carbohydrate:** 4 g

- **Cholesterol:** 18 mg
- **Total Fat:** 9.9 g

- **Fiber:** 4 g
- **Protein:** 14 g

55. QUICKLY COCONUT SPINACH

Easy/Dairy-free/Vegan
Preparation Time: 20 min
Cooking Time: 18 min

Servings: 2
- 2 cups spinach, chopped
- ½ cup coconut milk

- 1 tablespoon coconut oil
- ½ teaspoon nutmeg
- Salt and pepper to taste

Directions:
Take a skillet and heat the coconut oil on medium. Add chopped spinach and cook for 2 minutes, often stirring. Season with salt and pepper, pour the coconut milk and add nutmeg. Cook for 15 minutes, often stirring. Serve!

- **Calories:** 73
- **Carbohydrate:** 4 g
- **Cholesterol:** 0 mg
- **Total Fat:** 7 g
- **Fiber:** 4 g
- **Protein:** 4 g

56. CURRY SPINACH

Easy/Dairy-free/Vegan/Gluten-free
Preparation Time: 20 minutes
Cooking time: 15 minutes
Servings: 2
- 1-pound spinach, thawed
- 1 cup coconut milk
- 2 teaspoons yellow curry paste
- 1 teaspoon lemon zest
- 2 tablespoons walnuts, chopped
- Salt to taste

Directions:
Take a skillet and heat the curry paste on low for 1 minute, stirring. Add the coconut milk, little by little, and stir to combine. Cook for 5 minutes, until the paste is aromatic. Add the spinach, lemon zest, and a pinch of salt. Cook for 10 minutes, often stirring. Top with chopped nuts and serve!

- **Calories:** 191 kcal.
- **Net carbs**: 3 g
- **Protein:** 4 g
- **Fat:** 18 g

57. GARLIC CAULIFLOWER

Easy/Gluten-free/Vegan
Preparation Time: 20 minutes
Cooking time: 18 minutes
Servings: 4
Ingredients:
- 2 cups cauliflower
- 2 tablespoons olive oil
- 1 garlic clove, minced
- Salt and pepper to taste
- 1 tablespoon water
- 2 teaspoons lemon juice
- ½ teaspoon lemon zest
- 1 tablespoon chives, minced

Directions:
Take a skillet and heat olive oil on medium. Add cauliflower, minced garlic, lemon zest, lemon juice and a pinch of salt and pepper. Cook for 20 minutes, often stirring, until the cauliflower is almost mushy.
Take a food processor and add cauliflower mixture, chill and water. Blend until completely smooth. Serve.

- **Calories:** 178 kcal.
- **Net carbs:** 3 g,
- **Protein**: 2 g,
- **Fat:** 18g,

58. DELICIOUS LIME ASPARAGUS

Easy/Gluten-free/Vegan
Preparation time: 10 minutes
Cooking time: 8 minutes
Servings: 2

- 20 asparagus spears
- 2 garlic cloves, minced

- 1 tablespoon lime zest
- 1 tablespoon olive oil
- 2 tablespoons grated Parmesan cheese
- Salt and pepper to taste
- 2 tablespoons lime juice

Directions:

Preheat the oven to 400°F. Take a baking dish with a parchment paper.

Take a bowl and add coarsely chopped asparagus. Season with salt and pepper, pour lemon juice and mix well. Add minced garlic, lemon zest and olive oil. Stir to combine. Place asparagus into the baking dish. Sprinkle with Parmesan cheese and bake for 8 minutes. Enjoy!

59. SCRAMBLED EGGS AND SPINACH

Servings: 4
Cooking Time: 30 minutes
Ingredients:

- ½ red onion, chopped,
- 8 oz. spinach,

- 6 egg whites,
- 2 cloves of garlic chopped fine
- 1/4 cup feta cheese
- 2 tablespoons olive oil
- Salt and pepper to taste

Directions: In a skillet, heat on medium the olive oil. Sautee the spinach, garlic, and onion in skillet until spinach wilted. Whisk together the eggs and mix all the ingredients together with the cheese mixture. Add salt and pepper to taste and bake at 170°C for 30 minutes. Serve hot.

60. TASTY VEGGIE MIXTURE

Servings: 4
Cooking Time: 40 minutes
Ingredients:

- 2 cans of beans, rinsed and drained,
- 2 cups fresh tomatoes, diced,
- 1 ½ onions, chopped

- 1 cup of cauliflower
- ½ cup potatoes, chopped
- ¼ cup water
- 1 tbsp. mustard
- 3 tablespoons olive oil
- Salt and pepper to taste

Directions: In a large saucepan with cover, heat on medium the olive oil. Add the sliced onion and sauté for 2 minutes. Add chopped potatoes and beans and the water. Stir and cover. Cook for 15 minutes, stirring occasionally. Add more water if it needs. Season with salt and pepper. Then, reduce heat to low, add beans tomatoes and cauliflower, cover and cook 25 minutes. Stir occasionally and add more water if it needs. After, season if it needs, add mustard and mix well. Serve warm.

61. RATATOUILLE SOUP

Servings: 8
Cooking Time: 6 hours

Ingredients

- 2 cups sliced zucchini

- 1 chopped onion
- 2 sliced eggplants
- 1 sliced red pepper
- 2 tablespoons olive oil
- 2 garlic cloves, chopped
- Salt and pepper to taste

Instructions: Put ingredients in the pot. Cover, and cook on low for 6 hours. Serve warm.

62. BROWN RICE CARROTS AND MUSHROOMS STEW

Servings: 6
Cooking Time: 4 hours
Ingredients
- 2 chopped onions
- 2 tablespoons olive oil
- 1 sprig thyme, minced
- 4 chopped carrots
- 1 cup brown rice
- 2 cups mushrooms, sliced
- 4 cups vegetable stock
- Salt and pepper to taste
- 1 bunch chopped parsley

Instructions

Put all ingredients in a pot and cook on low for 4 hours. Stir occasionally. Serve warm.

63. VEGGIE MIX IN SOUP

Servings: 4
Cooking Time: 2 hours
Ingredients
- 2 cups sliced zucchini
- 2 cups sliced tomatoes
- 2 tablespoons olive oil
- 2 cups sliced eggplant
- salt and pepper to taste
- ½ garlic clove, minced

Instructions

Arrange all ingredients in a pot. Cover and cook on low for 2 hours. Stir occasionally. Serve warm.

64. VEGETARIAN CHILI

Servings: 6
Cooking Time: 5 hours
Ingredients
- 1 tablespoon olive oil
- 1 cup chopped onions
- 1/2 cup chopped carrots
- 2 garlic cloves, minced
- 1/2 chopped green bell pepper
- 1/2 chopped red bell pepper
- 1/2 cup chopped celery
- 1 tablespoons chili powder
- 1 cup chopped mushrooms
- 3 cups chopped tomatoes
- 2 cups raw kidney beans
- 1 tablespoons ground cumin
- 1/2 teaspoon oregano
- 1/2 teaspoon minced basil leaves

Instructions: Put all ingredients in a pot. Cook on low for 5 hours, stirring occasionally. Serve warm

65. GLUTEN-FREE FETA PIZZA

Servings: 2
Cooking Time: 15 minutes
Ingredients:
- 1 pre-baked gluten-free pizza crust
- 4 slices Feta cheese
- 3 tablespoons olive oil

- 2 cloves of garlic, minced
- 2 teaspoons fresh oregano, chopped

Directions:

Preheat oven to 375°F. Take a regular baking sheet or a round pan. To prepare the dish, brush each crust with olive oil and sprinkle minced garlic all over the crust. Place the turkey slices evenly and sprinkle herbs on pizza crust. Bake in preheated oven for about 10-12 minutes and crust is golden brown.

66. <u>VERY SPICY POTATOES</u>

Servings: 2

Cooking Time: 20 minutes

- 4 cups potatoes, chopped
- 2 teaspoons paprika
- Salt and pepper to taste
- 1 teaspoon cumin
- 1 teaspoon fennel
- 2 teaspoons ginger
- 1 teaspoon chili powder
- 2 tablespoons olive oil

Directions:

In a bowl, combine the potatoes and ½ tbsp. oil. In another bowl, mix the ground cumin, ginger, fennel, paprika, chili powder and salt. Put this mixture over the potatoes and toss well until they're fully coated. Place the potatoes on an aluminum foil and seal the packet.

Grill the potatoes in foil for 20 minutes, until they are well-cooked and look tender. Drizzle the potatoes with the remaining olive oil and then transfer them to a serving bowl. Serve warm, with chicken or salmon.

67. <u>DELICIOUS TOMATO SOUP</u>

Servings: 4

Cooking Time: 35 minutes

- 4 cups tomatoes, chopped
- 2 teaspoons butter
- Salt and pepper to taste
- 2 mint leaves
- 1 teaspoon ground coriander
- 3 cups water

Directions: Put the tomatoes in boiling water for 5 minutes. Transfer them to ice-cold water immediately. Peel the skins and cut the tomatoes into small pieces. Take water in a pan, let it boil. Add the chopped tomatoes. Add mint and salt to the boiling mixture. Boil for about 20 minutes. Allow it to cool and blend the tomatoes with the help of a mixer. Sieve the blended mixture to remove the seeds. Garnish it with a dash of butter and coriander leaves. Serve hot.

68. <u>TASTY PUMPKIN AND GINGER SOUP</u>

Servings: 2

Cooking Time: 1 hour

- 2 tablespoons olive oil
- 1 onion, diced
- 2 teaspoons ginger root
- 4 cups butternut squash
- 4 cups chicken broth
- Salt and pepper to taste

Directions:

1.Cut the squash, take out the seeds and place in the oven on a cookie sheet; bake for approx. 1 hour at 170°C. After, heat the oil in a large pot on low. Add onion and ginger and cook until softened. Remove onion and ginger from the heat and place them in a food processor. Add in cooked squash, chicken broth and blend until uniform. Add the mixture to pot from before and reheat for 2 minutes. Season and serve.

69. <u>VERY SUPER CHILI</u>

Servings: 6
Cooking Time: 4 hours
Ingredients

- 2 tablespoons olive oil
- 2 onions, chopped
- 3 garlic cloves, minced
- 2 cups bread slices, cubed
- 2 cups diced tomatoes
- 1 cup tomato paste
- 1 tablespoons cumin seeds
- 1 tablespoon cocoa powder
- 1 teaspoon ground coriander
- Salt and pepper to taste
- 6 cups cooked kidney beans
- 4 fresh hot chili peppers, chopped

Instructions

Put all ingredients in a pot. Cover and cook on low for 4 hours. Stir frequently. Serve warm.

70. <u>PEAS AND CARROTS SOUP</u>

Servings: 8
Cooking Time: 6 hours
Ingredients

- 3 large chopped carrots
- 1 large chopped onion
- 2 tablespoons olive oil
- 1 garlic clove minced
- 2 cups green peas
- 4 cups vegetables stock
- Salt and pepper to taste
- 2 cups spinach, chopped

Instructions: Put all ingredients in a pot. Cover and cook on low for 6 hours. Serve warm.

71. <u>AWESOME VEGGIES BALLS</u>

Preparation Time: 15 Minutes
Cooking Time: 30 Minutes
Servings: 6
FOR THE BALLS:

- 2 cups Ricotta cheese
- ½ cup almond flour
- ½ cup Parmesan cheese
- 1 egg, beaten
- 1 tablespoon chopped fresh parsley
- 1 teaspoon minced garlic
- 1 teaspoon chopped fresh oregano
- Salt and pepper to taste
- 2 tablespoons olive oil
- 2 potatoes, peeled

FOR THE PARMIGIANA:

- 1 cup sugar-free tomato sauce
- 1 cup shredded mozzarella cheese

Directions:

<u>To make the Balls:</u>

Take a pot and bring the water to a boil. Season with salt and add chopped potatoes. Boil them for 15 minutes, then drain.

In a large bowl, mix together cooked potatoes, almond flour, Parmesan, egg, parsley, garlic, Ricotta cheese, oregano, salt, and pepper until everything is well mixed. Roll the mixture into 1½-inch balls.

Take a large skillet and heat the olive oil on medium. Add the balls to the skillet and cook them, turning them several times, until they're completely cooked through, about 15 minutes in total.

To make the Parmigiana:

1. Preheat the oven. Set the oven temperature to 350°F.

2. Assemble the parmigiana. Transfer the balls to a 9-by-9-inch baking dish and top them with the tomato sauce. Sprinkle with the mozzarella and bake for 15 minutes or until the cheese is melted and golden. Serve. Divide the balls and sauce between six bowls and serve it immediately.

72. PEANUT NOODLES

Servings: 4

Cooking time: 20 minutes

Preparation Time: 10 minutes

Ingredients

- √ 4 ounces noodles
- √ 2 cucumbers sliced
- √ 2 scallions, sliced
- √ 1/2 cup chopped fresh cilantro
- √ 1/2 cup shelled edamame
- √ 1 tablespoon toasted sesame seeds

PEANUT SAUCE INGREDIENTS:

- √ 1/4 cup natural peanut butter
- √ 2 tablespoons lime juice
- √ 2 tablespoons white vinegar
- √ 1 tablespoon honey
- √ 1 tablespoon toasted sesame oil
- √ 1/2 teaspoon ginger

Directions:

Take a pot and bring the water to a boil. Cook the soba noodles al dente for 10 minutes. Drain and set aside on the table for 10 minutes.

Meanwhile, take a bowl and whisk together all of the peanut sauce ingredients until combined. Add to the sauce cucumbers, scallions, cilantro and edamame. Mix well. Once noodles are cooked, add them to the bowl and mix with the sauce. Serve immediately, sprinkled with toasted sesame seeds.

73. TRADITIONAL RATATOUILLE

Servings: 4

Cooking time: 30 minutes

Preparation Time: 30 minutes

Ingredients

- √ 1 medium eggplant, chopped
- √ Salt and pepper
- √ 3 tablespoons olive oil, divided
- √ 1 white onion, chopped
- √ 3 garlic cloves, chopped
- √ 2 bell peppers, cored and chopped
- √ 1 zucchini, sliced
- √ 2 cups cherry tomatoes
- √ 4 basil leaves
- √ 1/4 teaspoon red pepper flakes
- √ 1 bay leaf
- √ 2 sprigs fresh thyme
- √ 1/2 cup red wine

Directions:

Add diced eggplant to a colander, and toss with 1 teaspoon salt. Let sit 15 minutes, then rinse and drain.

Meanwhile, in a pot, heat 1 tablespoon oil on medium. Add onion and sauté for 5 minutes, stirring occasionally. Add the remaining 2 tablespoons olive oil, garlic, sliced bell peppers, and zucchini, and sauté for an additional 10 minutes, stirring occasionally, until the vegetables are mostly cooked through.

Stir in the eggplant, chopped tomatoes, basil leaves, red pepper flakes, bay leaf, and rosemary, and cook for 8 more minutes, stirring occasionally. Slowly add in the wine, stir and cook for 5 minutes. Season, and remove the bay leaf and rosemary. Serve warm.

74. GAZPACHO

Servings: 4
Cooking time: 0 minutes
Preparation Time: 3 hours
Ingredients

- √ 2 cups tomatoes, diced
- √ 1 cucumber, peeled and chopped
- √ 1 yellow bell pepper, cored
- √ 1 small red onion, peeled
- √ 2 garlic cloves, peeled
- √ 3 tablespoons olive oil
- √ 2 tablespoons white vinegar
- √ Salt and pepper to taste
- √ 1/2 teaspoon cumin

Directions:

Combine all ingredients together in a blender or food processor. Blend for 1 minute, until it is smooth. Taste and season with extra salt, pepper and/or cumin if needed. Cover with a plastic wrap and refrigerate for 3 hours. Serve cold, topped with your desired garnishes.

75. DELICIOUS SPINACH AND POTATOES BALLS

Preparation Time: 10 minutes
Cooking Time: 40 minutes
Servings: 3

- √ 4 medium potatoes
- √ 2 cups fresh spinach
- √ 4 cloves garlic, minced
- √ 2 tablespoons vegetable broth
- √ 5 fresh basil leaves
- √ 1 tablespoon dried Parsley
- √ 1/2 teaspoon ground cumin
- √ 1/2 cup breadcrumbs

Directions

1. Wash and quarter 4 medium potatoes and add to a large pot. Add enough cold water to cover and bring to a boil. Add a pinch of salt and let boil for 5 minutes. Take a skillet and add broth with garlic. Heat on medium for 5 minutes, frequently stirring. Drain potatoes and mash them in the skillet.

2. Meanwhile, wash and chop the fresh spinach. Add spinach and remaining seasonings and mix well. Cook for 10 minutes. Once mixture is cool down, add into breadcrumbs and mix. Form 15-20 balls.

3. Preheat oven at 450°F. Place the balls in a baking dish and cook for 20 minutes. Serve warm.

76. BASIL LEMON RATATOUILLE

Preparation Time: 35 minutes
Cooking Time: 30 minutes
Servings: 4
√ 1 eggplant, cut into cubes
√ 5 leaves of fresh basil
√ 2 cups cherry tomatoes, chopped
√ 1 onion, chopped
√ 2 zucchinis, sliced

√ 2 tablespoons vinegar
√ 1 tablespoon tomato paste
√ 2 garlic cloves, minced
√ 3 tablespoons olive oil
√ Salt to taste
√ 1 cup of water
√ 1 fresh lemon juice

Directions

1. Take your food processor. Add basil, vinegar, tomato paste, garlic, lemon juice, oil, and salt into the blender and blend until smooth. Take a non-stick pot and heat olive oil on medium. Add onion and cook for 3-4 minutes. Add to pot eggplant, tomatoes, water, and zucchini. Cook for 15 minutes, occasionally stirring. Pour blended basil mixture into the pot and stir well. Continue to cook for 10 minutes, seasoning with salt. Once done, let it rest for 20 minutes. Stir well and serve.

77. POTATOES OMELETS

Preparation Time: 10 minutes
Cooking Time: 38 minutes
Servings: 2
√ 2 eggs, beaten
√ 1 garlic clove

√ ½ teaspoon chives minced
√ 2 potatoes, peeled
√ 2 tablespoons olive oil
√ Salt to taste

Directions: Take a pot and bring the water to a boil. Add a pinch of salt and potatoes. Cook for 20 minutes. Mix together eggs, a pinch of salt and chives using a fork. Season with salt. Once potatoes are cooked, take a skillet and heat on medium olive oil. Chop garlic and add in the skillet. Cook for 2 minutes stirring. Add chopped potatoes and cook for 10 minutes. Pour the egg mixture into the skillet and flatten it. Cover with the lid. Cook omelet for 5 minutes on each side over low heat. Serve warm!

78. CAULIFLOWER QUINOA

Preparation Time: 15 minutes
Cooking Time: 10 minutes
Servings: 4
√ 2 cups of pre-cooked quinoa

√ 3 tablespoons olive oil
√ 3 cups cauliflower florets
√ 1 onion, chopped
√ 1 tablespoon red wine

√ Salt and pepper to taste

√ 1 tablespoon chives, chopped

√ 1 tablespoon parsley, chopped

Directions:

1. Heating a pan over medium heat and add olive oil. Once the oil is hot, add the onion and cook for 2 minutes. Add quinoa and cauliflower and stir gently. After 2 minutes, add the rest of the ingredients. Mix well and cook at low heat for 5-6 minutes, covering with the lid. Serve warm.

79. <u>TOFU WITH MUSHROOMS</u>

Preparation Time: 5 minutes
Cooking Time: 10 minutes
Servings: 2

√ 1 cup fresh mushrooms, chopped finely

√ 1 cup tofu, cubed into 1-inch pieces

√ 4 tablespoons butter

√ Salt and black pepper, to taste

√ 4 tablespoons Parmesan cheese, shredded

Directions

1. Season the tofu with salt and black pepper. Take a skillet and melt on low the butter, then add tofu and cook for 5 minutes. Add mushrooms and Parmesan cheese and cook for another 5 minutes, stirring occasionally. Dish out and serve immediately.

80. <u>BAKED EGGS AND ASPARAGUS WITH PARMESAN</u>

Preparation Time: 10 minutes
Cooking Time: 18 minutes
Servings: 2

√ 4 eggs

√ 8 thick asparagus spears

√ 4 tablespoons olive oil to grease the pans

√ 2 tablespoons Parmesan cheese, grated

√ Salt and black pepper, to taste

Directions

1. Preheat the oven to 400° F. Grease two baking dishes with olive oil.

2. Cut asparagus into bite-sized pieces. Put half the asparagus into each baking dish and place it in the oven. Roast for 10 minutes and remove them from the oven, letting them rest.

4. Crack eggs in a plate, add the rest of the asparagus and mix well with a fork. Add salt and pepper to taste. Transfer the eggs into each baking dish with cooked asparagus. Bake for 5 minutes. Remove the baking dishes from the oven and sprinkle the eggs with Parmesan. Put the eggs back in the oven. Bake for another 3 minutes. Dish out immediately to serve hot.

81. <u>RED WINE RISOTTO</u>

Preparation Time: 10 minutes
Cooking Time: 25 minutes
Servings: 8

√ Pepper and salt to taste

√ 1 cup of Parmesan, grated

√ 1 tablespoon tomato paste

√ 2 cups red wine

√ 2 cups brown rice

√ 2 cloves garlic, minced

√ 1 medium onion, freshly chopped

√ 2 tablespoons extra-virgin olive oil

√ 4 cups veggies broth

Directions

1. In a large pan heat the oil on medium. Sauté garlic and onions for 5-6 minutes. Stir frequently. Pour 2 cups of broth into the pan and bring it to a simmer. Lower fire so the broth is steaming but not simmering. Add rice, mix well, and season with salt and pepper, and simmer for 10 minutes. Pour 1 cup of red wine and cook until liquid is fully absorbed, frequently stirring. Add another 1 cup of wine and 2 cups of broth. Stirring once in a while. Add tomato paste and stir to mix well. Continue cooking and adding wine and broth until broth is used up. Once done cooking, turn off the fire and stir in pepper and ¾ cup cheese. To serve, sprinkle with remaining cheese and enjoy.

82. SCOTCH EGGS

Ingredients:
- √ 4 eggs
- √ 1 teaspoon rosemary
- √ ¼ teaspoon nutmeg
- √ ½ teaspoon garlic powder
- √ ½ teaspoon onion powder
- √ 1 cup spinach

Dairy-free - **Servings:** 2
Preparation Time: 30 minutes
Cooking Time: 30 minutes
- Pepper and salt
- ¼ teaspoon crushed red pepper

ALMOND MEAL CRUST:
- √ 1 egg
- √ ¼ cup almond milk
- √ ⅓ cup almond meal
- √ Salt

Directions: Oven: 425°F.

Boil your eggs anywhere from 9 minutes. After cooking, peel them
Combine the seasonings with the chopped spinaches in a bowl. Separate the seasoned spinach into four equal parts. In a separate bowl, the almond milk and egg must be combined. In another container or bowl, combine the salt and almond meal. Take the spinach and shape into a patty then take the boiled egg and mold the spinach around the egg, making sure no egg white is showing through.
Dip each covered egg in the egg wash; almond meal until completely covered.
Bake for 25–30 minutes or until the outer crust is browned. Serve.

83. EGG AND HASH BROWN CUPS

Ingredients:
- √ 3 cups grated potatoes
- √ ½ teaspoon salt
- √ 5 eggs
- √ ½ teaspoon thyme
- √ ¼ teaspoon red pepper
- √ Black pepper
- √ Ketchup, for serving

Dairy-free
Preparation Time: 15 minutes
Cooking Time: 30 minutes
Servings: 5
Difficulty: Medium

Directions: Oven: 425°F

Grease muffin pans then place the grated potatoes in the muffin slots and gently press the potatoes down, creating a cup. Season with salt and bake for 15 minutes. Crack each egg into the hash brown cups then top with remaining seasonings. Bake for 15 minutes. Serve with Ketchup.

84. <u>BLACKBERRIES COFFEE CAKE</u>

Ingredients:

FOR THE BATTER

- √ ¼ teaspoon coconut oil
- √ 1½ cups gluten-free flour
- √ ½ cup granulated sugar
- √ 2 large eggs
- √ ½ cup coconut milk
- √ 2 tablespoons sunflower oil

FOR THE STREUSEL

- √ ⅔ cup almond flour
- √ ½ cup granulated sugar
- √ 1½ teaspoons cinnamon

Preparation Time: 15 minutes
Cooking Time: 25 minutes
Servings: 8
Difficulty: Medium

- √ Juice of 1 lemon
- √ 1 cup blackberries

- √ ¼ cup dairy-free butter
- √ Lemon Zest

Directions: Oven: 325°F. The pan must then be greased with the oil.

For the batter: Stir together all the batter ingredients. Gently fold in the blueberries then pour into the baking pan. Meanwhile, in a bowl or container all streusel ingredients. Top the batter with the streusel, gently pressing it into the batter. Bake for 20 to 25 minutes.

85. <u>THE BEST BERRY CHEESECAKE</u>

Ingredients:

CRUST

- √ 6 tablespoons nondairy butter
- √ 1 cup gluten-free rolled oats
- √ 1 cup tapioca flour

Dairy-free
Preparation Time: 40 minutes
Cooking Time: 10 minutes
Servings: 12
Difficulty: Hard

√ 1 cup dry unsweetened coconut
√ 6 tablespoons maple syrup
√ Salt

GELATIN MIX:
√ ½ cup of water
√ 1½ teaspoons agar-agar

FILLING AND TOPPING
√ ½ teaspoon salt
√ 16 ounces non-dairy cream cheese
√ ½ cup canned coconut milk
√ 1 tablespoon nutritional yeast
√ 1 teaspoon vanilla extract
√ ⅔ cup honey
√ Topping:
√ 1½ cups mixed berries

Directions: Oven: 350°F

In a food processor, pulse all crust ingredients. Press the mixture onto the base of the springform pan. Let the cheesecake bake for 10 minutes while preparing the filling. Set aside. For the filling: In a heated saucepan, combine the salt and water and sprinkle with gelatin then bring to a boil. In a container, beat all filling ingredients. Incorporate the gelatin mixture then blend well. Pour this to the crust and until firm. Garnish with berries and drizzled with honey.

86. SIMPLE CAKE

Ingredients:

DRY INGREDIENTS:
√ 2 cups gluten-free flour
√ ¼ cup arrowroot
√ 1 tablespoon baking powder
√ 1 teaspoon xanthan gum
√ ¼ teaspoon salt

WET INGREDIENTS:
√ 1 cup honey
√ 1 cup vegan butter
√ 4 large eggs

Preparation Time: 15 minutes
Cooking Time: 60 minutes
Servings: 12
Difficulty: Medium

√ 1 teaspoon vinegar
√ 1 teaspoon vanilla extract
√ ¼ cup sour cream

TOPPING:
√ Confectioners' sugar

Directions: Oven: 350°F. Take a grease 9" pan.

In a bowl, mix all dry ingredients. In another bowl, beat the honey and butter together until fluffy. Beat in remaining wet ingredients. Bake it for about 1 hour. Dust with confectioners' sugar before serving.

87. ZUCCHINI BUNDT CAKE

Ingredients:
DRY INGREDIENTS:
- √ 3 cups gluten-free flour
- √ 1 tablespoon baking powder
- √ 1½ teaspoons cinnamon
- √ 1½ teaspoons xanthan gum
- √ 1 teaspoon baking soda
- √ 1 teaspoon salt

WET INGREDIENTS:
- √ 3 large eggs
- √ 1 cup coconut sugar
- √ 1 cup avocado oil
- √ ½ cup maple syrup
- √ 1 tablespoon vanilla extract
- √ 2 cups grated zucchini
- √ ½ cup chopped walnuts

Dairy-free
Preparation Time: 15 minutes
Cooking Time: 55 minutes
Servings: 12
Difficulty: Medium

Directions: Oven: 350°F. Coat a 9-inch Bundt pan with cooking spray and flour.
In a bowl all dry ingredients must be combined. In a second bowl, beat the eggs until light and creamy. Beat in the remaining dry ingredients. Fold in the walnuts. Pour into the pan and bake for 55 minutes.

88. NO-BAKE BERRY CHEESECAKE

Ingredients:
CRUST:
- √ 2 cups gluten-free pretzels

- √ 1 tablespoon brown sugar
- √ ½ cup melted vegan butter/ coconut oil

FILLING:
- √ 2 packages cream cheese
- √ 1 cup sour cream

TOPPING:
- √ 1 can gluten-free berry pie filling

Preparation Time: 15 minutes
Cooking Time: 25 minutes

Servings: 9
Difficulty: Easy

- √ 1 cup powdered sugar
- √ 1 teaspoon vanilla extract

Directions:
Pulse all the crust mixture then press into an 8-by-8-inch baking dish.
In a container, whip all filling ingredients. Spread this mixture over the crust. Let it freeze for 15 more minutes. Spread the cherry pie filling over the cheesecake.

89. RICE WITH EGG, CARROTS AND PEAS

- √ 1 medium red onion, diced
- √ 2 tablespoons olive oil
- √ 2 carrots, finely cubed
- √ 1 ½ cups vegetable broth
- √ 1 can of peas (drained)
- √ 2 cups dry white rice
- √ 4 eggs
- √ Salt and pepper to taste

Directions:

1. In a large skillet heat the olive oil on medium.
2. Put the peas and cook for 15 minutes, adding salt and pepper. Add the broth and the cubed carrots and cook for 15 minutes on low heat.
3. Meanwhile, take a pot and bring the water to a boil. Add a pinch of salt to the water and add the rice. Cook on medium heat for 20 minutes.
4. Once the rice is cooked, drain it and add it to the skillet with carrots and peas, without turn off the heat. Add the eggs to the skillet. Cook all the ingredients on low heat, stirring frequently, for 10 minutes. Once the eggs are cooked, turn off the heat and serve immediately!

Preparation Time: 10 minutes	
Cooking Time: 40 minutes	
Servings: 4	

90. RICE AND CURRANT SALAD

- √ 1 cup basmati rice
- √ Salt
- √ 2 1/2 tablespoons lemon juice
- √ 1 teaspoon grated orange zest
- √ 2 tablespoons fresh orange juice
- √ 1/4 cup olive oil
- √ 1/2 teaspoon cinnamon
- √ Salt and pepper to taste
- √ 4 chopped green onions
- √ 1/2 cup dried currants
- √ 10 shelled almonds, minced (optional)
- √ 10 leaves of fresh parsley, chopped

Preparation Time: 40 minutes
Cooking Time: 20 minutes
Servings: 4

Directions

1. Place a large nonstick pot on medium high fire and add rice. Toast rice until opaque and start to brown, for 10 minutes.
2. Meanwhile bring the water to a boil on medium heat.
3. Add 4 cups of boiling water to pot and 2 tablespoons of salt. Boil until tender, around 8 minutes uncovered. Drain the rice and spread out on a lined cookie sheet to cool completely.
4. In a large salad bowl, whisk well the oil, juices and spices. Add salt and pepper to taste.

5. Add green onions, parsley leaves, currants, and almonds.
6. Toss with the cooled rice and let stand for at least 20 minutes. Enjoy!

91. <u>POTATO SALAD</u>

√ 6 potatoes
√ 2 tablespoons olive oil
√ 2 scallions, thinly sliced
√ Ground pepper to taste
√ 2 tablespoons lemon juice
√ salt to taste
√ 2 tablespoons mint leaves, chopped

Preparation Time: 5 minutes
Cooking Time: 10 minutes
Servings: 4

Directions

1. Place a saucepan half filled with water over medium heat. Add salt and potatoes and cook for 15 minutes. Drain the potatoes and place in a bowl of cold water. When cool enough to handle, peel and cube the potatoes and let them rest in the bowl.

2. Add oil, lemon juice, salt and pepper in a separate bowl and whisk well. Drizzle dressing over the potatoes. Toss well. Add scallions and mint and toss well. Enjoy!

92. <u>SIMPLE SAFFRON RISOTTO</u>

√ 2 cups vegetable broth
√ 2 tablespoon butter
√ 1 tablespoon olive oil
√ 1 red onion, very finely chopped
√ 2 cups of rice
√ 1 cup of white wine
√ 1 tablespoon saffron
√ 2 Tablespoons of Parmesan, grated
√ 1 egg yolk
√ Salt to taste

Preparation Time: 5 minutes
Cooking Time: 35 minutes
Servings: 4

Directions

1. Take a pot and heat the broth on low.
2. Take a large non-stick pan and melt the butter; then add onion and a large salt pinch. Cook, frequently stirring, for 5 minutes until softened and fragrant.

3. Put in the pan the rice and mix it with butter and onion. Add 4 tablespoons of warm broth, cooking for 10 minutes until it is absorbed.

4. Add 1 tablespoon of olive oil and the rest of the broth little by little to rice. Stir and continue to cook. Pour in the wine and cook, stirring, until it is absorbed. Add the saffron and stir. After 25-30 mins, all the broth should be absorbed. Add the Parmesan and stir continuously until melted. Turn off the heat and stir in the egg yolk. Season with salt. Serve immediately!

93. CHEESE TORTELLINI

- √ 16 ounces Ricotta cheese Tortellini
- √ 1 teaspoon minced garlic
- √ 1 can peeled tomatoes
- √ 2 tablespoons whole flour
- √ 1 cup chopped fresh spinach
- √ ¼ cup milk
- √ Salt and pepper to taste
- √ ½ cup heavy cream
- √ ¼ cup grated Parmesan cheese
- √ 3 fresh basil leaves

Servings: 6	
Preparation Time: 20 minutes	
Cooking Time: 20 minutes	

Directions

1. Take a pot and bring the water to a boil. Season with salt and add Tortellini. Cook for 5 minutes.

2. Meanwhile take a skillet and add peeled tomatoes and heat on medium for 5 minutes; crush them with a fork while they are cooking. Stir in spinach, salt, pepper, chopped basil leaves and garlic. Cook for 10 minutes, often stirring.

3. In another bowl, whisk together the whole flour, milk and cream. Stir this mixture into the skillet, mix gently. Add the Parmesan cheese and cook on low for 5 minutes, constantly stirring to avoid cheese lumps. Drain the Tortellini. Stir to coat and serve.

94. SPICY SPINACH AND CARROTS

- √ 12 ounces penne pasta
- √ 2 cups spinach, chopped
- √ ¼ cup butter
- √ 1 can tomato sauce
- √ 2 tablespoons extra-virgin olive oil
- √ ½ cup grated Parmesan cheese
- √ 1 white onion, diced
- √ ½ cup sour cream
- √ 3 garlic cloves, minced
- √ 1 red bell pepper, diced

Servings: 6	
Preparation Time: 30 minutes	
Cooking Time: 20 minutes	

- √ Salt and pepper to taste
- √ ½ pound mushrooms, diced
- √ ¼ cup chopped parsley
- √ 2 carrots

Directions

Take a pot and bring the water to a boil. Season with salt and add pasta; cook for 10 minutes or until al dente; drain. Meanwhile, take a skillet and melt on low the butter; add olive oil and cook for 2 minutes on medium. Stir in sliced onion, garlic cloves, red pepper and cook for 3 minutes, often stirring. Add mushrooms and cook for another 6 minutes, often stirring. Stir in the chopped carrots, and cook for 10 minutes, frequently stirring. Pour in the skillet tomato sauce, Parmesan cheese, spinach, and sour cream; bring to a simmer for 10 minutes, stirring constantly. Season with a pinch of salt and pepper. Stir drained pasta into the sauce and serve sprinkled with chopped parsley.

95. PAN-FRIED ASPARAGUS

- √ 1/4 cup butter
- √ Salt and pepper to taste
- √ 2 tablespoons olive oil
- √ 3 cloves garlic, minced
- √ 1-pound fresh asparagus spears, trimmed

| Servings: 4 |
| Preparation Time: 5 minutes |
| Cooking Time: 15 minutes |

Directions

1. Melt butter in a skillet over medium-high heat. Stir in the olive oil, salt, and pepper. Cook garlic in butter for 2 minutes, but do not brown. Add asparagus, and cook for 10 minutes, turning asparagus to ensure even cooking. Enjoy!

96. VEGETARIAN PIZZA

- √ 1/2 cups warm water
- √ 1/2 teaspoons of yeast
- √ 4 cups bread flour
- √ tablespoons extra virgin olive oil
- √ 2 teaspoons salt
- √ 1 teaspoon sugar
- √ a bit of flour to knead

FOR TOPPING:
- √ Extra virgin olive oil
- √ 1 can of Tomato sauce
- √ 1 cup of Mozzarella cheese, crumbled

- √ 2 tablespoons Fontina cheese, grated
- √ 2 tablespoons Parmesan cheese, grated
- √ 1/2 cup of Mushrooms, very thinly sliced
- √ 1/2 Bell pepper, stems and seeds removed, very thinly sliced
- √ 8 black olives, Sliced
- √ 4 leaves of fresh basil, chopped
- √ 1 red onion, thinly sliced
- √ Salt and pepper to taste

Preparation Time: 3 hours 30 minutes	
Cooking Time: 10 minutes	
Servings: 2	

Directions

1. Place the warm water in a large bowl. Sprinkle the yeast over the warm water and let it sit for 5 minutes until the yeast is dissolved. Stir if the yeast hasn't dissolved completely.

2. Add 4 cups of flour, salt, sugar, and olive oil, gently mix for 1 minute, using a fork or the mixing paddle attachment.

3. Once mix are uniform, sprinkle a bit of flour on the table and knead the pizza dough by hand. your hand for 20-25 minutes. The dough should be a little sticky, or tacky to the touch. If it's too wet, sprinkle in a little more flour. It it's too dry add a bit of warm water.

4. In a large bowl, spread a thin layer of olive oil on the bottom and place the pizza dough in the bowl and turn it around so that it gets coated with the oil. Cover the dough with plastic wrap and let it rest for 2 hours and 30 minutes on room temperature.

5. Preheat the oven to 475°F.

6. Take your dough. Dust your hands with flour and gently handle the dough for 2 minutes.

7. Divide it in half and form two round balls. Place each in two different bowls, cover with plastic and let sit for 20 minutes.

8. Work one ball of dough at a time. Take one ball of dough and flatten it with your hands on a lightly floured work surface. Starting at the center and working outwards, use your fingertips to press the dough to 1/2-inch thick. Turn and stretch the dough until it will not stretch further. Once they are made, let them rest 5 minutes. Then continue to stretch them very gently until it reaches the desired diameter (about 10 inches).

9. Brush the top of each pizza with a bit of olive oil. Let them rest another 10 minutes.

10. Pour 1/2 can of tomatoes on each pizza top. Sprinkle a pinch of salt and pepper and a little bit of oil on the tomato. Sprinkle 1 tablespoon Fontina, 1/2 cup of Mozzarella, 1 tablespoon of Parmesan, 4 sliced olives and 2 minced leaves of basil on each pizza. Top with half of sliced mushrooms, half of sliced bell pepper and half of sliced onion on each pizza.

11. Bake pizza for 8-10 minutes. Enjoy!

97. VEGETABLES LASAGNA

- √ 2 tablespoons olive oil
- √ 1 red onion

√ 1 clove garlic

√ 10 leaves fresh parsley

√ 1 large carrot

√ 2 pounds of ground beef

√ 2 tablespoons tomato paste

√ 2 cans of peeled tomatoes

√ 10 leaves of fresh basil

       For Cream:

√ 2 teaspoons of salt

√ 1 teaspoon black pepper

√ 1 can dried peas

√ 1-pound Lasagna sheets

√ 2 oz Parmesan cheese, grated

| Preparation Time: 20 minutes |
| Cooking Time: 1 hour 20 minutes |
| Servings: 4 |

✓ 5 teaspoons psyllium husk powder

✓ 2 cups sour cream

✓ 1 cup feta cheese, crumbled

✓ 1/2 cup almond milk

Directions:

1. Mince the garlic and the onion.

2. Heat on medium the olive oil in a pot. Add garlic and onion and sauté for 2-3 minutes stirring frequently. Chop the carrot and the fresh parsley and add them to the pot.

3. Add peeled tomatoes, peas, tomato paste, and basil leaves to the pot, seasoning with salt and pepper. Stir gently. Cover and cook on low for 1 hour. Add some water if the sauce needs it.

4. Meanwhile, take a pot and bring the water to a boil. Put in the lasagna sheets and cook for 5 minutes. Remove the sheets from the water and lay them all out, covering the table: let them rest for 10 minutes.

5. Meanwhile, in a bowl combine the psyllium husk powder, sour cream, feta cheese and almond milk. Mix very well to make a uniform cream.

6. Preheat your oven to 400°F.

7. Once the sauce is ready, turn off the heat and take a baking dish. Add the first layer of tomato sauce, then cover with lasagna sheets. Put the second layer of sauce and mix with the first layer of cream. Sprinkle Parmesan cheese. Cover with another layer of Lasagna sheets. Continue until you finish the pasta, cream and sauce. Topping with the last layer of sauce mixed with the cream and the last sprinkle of Parmesan. Bake for 20 minutes. Serve warm!

98. LENTILS PASTA

√ 2 tablespoons olive oil

√ 1 onion, chopped

√ 1 tablespoon chopped garlic

√ 2 medium carrots, peeled, and sliced

| Preparation Time: 20 minutes |
| Cooking Time: 55 minutes |
| Servings: 4 |

- √ 8 ounces mushrooms, chopped
- √ 2 tablespoons tomato paste
- √ 1 can no-salt-added crushed tomatoes
- √ 1 cup uncooked brown lentils
- √ 8 ounces whole-wheat penne pasta
- √ 1 teaspoon dried laurel
- √ ½ cup red wine
- √ 2 cups water
- √ ½ teaspoon salt

Directions

Heat on medium 1 tablespoon of olive oil in a pot. Add the onion, and garlic and cook for 2 minutes. Add the carrots and mushrooms, then stir and cook for another 5 minutes.

Add the laurel and tomato paste, stir to evenly incorporate, and cook for 5 more minutes, without stirring. Add the wine. Stir and cook for 2 more minutes. Add crushed tomatoes, water, lentils, and salt. Bring to a boil, then turn the heat down to low and simmer for 40 minutes. Meanwhile, take another pot an bring the water to a boil. Season with salt and cook the pasta for 10 minutes. Drain pasta, and combine with the sauce, stir in the remaining 1 tablespoon of oil and. Serve!

99. EGG CAPRESE

- √ ½ garlic clove, minced
- √ 2 basil leaves, sliced
- √ 12 Mozzarella balls
- √ 3 cups spinach
- √ 12 large eggs
- √ 2 cups chopped tomatoes
- √ Salt and pepper to taste

Preparation Time: 20 minutes	
Cooking Time: 17 minutes	
Servings: 8	

- √ 2 tablespoons Parmesan, grated
- √ 1 tablespoon Balsamic vinegar

Directions

1. Preheat the oven to 350°F.

2. Take a muffin pan and make a layer of spinach at the bottom of each cup. Arrange tomatoes, mozzarella, and basil above the spinach layer.

3. In a bowl, mix the eggs, Parmesan, garlic minced and salt and pepper pinch. Add the egg mixture into muffin cups. Bake for 20 minutes.

4. Pour a bit of balsamic vinegar and serve!

100. DELICIOUS TOMATO AND FETA COUSCOUS

- √ 1 ½ cups couscous
- √ 1 teaspoon powdered vegetable stock
- √ 1½ cups boiled water
- √ 1 garlic clove, minced

Preparation Time: 15 minutes	
Cooking Time: 10 minutes	
Servings: 6	

- √　　1 can sun-dried tomato
- √　　1 can of chickpeas, dried
- √　　1 teaspoon coriander powder
- √　　½ cup chopped coriander
- √　　1 red onion, chopped
- √　　½ cup chopped parsley
- ✓ Lemon zest
- ✓ ½ cup arugula lettuce
- ✓ Salt and pepper to taste
- ✓ 5 tablespoons lemon juice
- ✓ ½ cup feta cheese, crumbled

Directions

1. In a large bowl, combine garlic, chickpeas, stock powder, couscous, and coriander. Add hot water to the bowl and mix well. Cover the bowl and keep it aside for 10 minutes.

2. Add to the bowl the tomatoes, lemon juice, coriander, pepper, parsley, salt, onions, and lemon zest and toss well. Sprinkle the feta cheese and serve!

CONCLUSION

Thank you for reading "*The Plant-Based Cookbook*"!

I hope you found a lot of tasty recipes!

I wish you to achieve all your goals!

Caroline Lewis